This journal belongs to:

_____

Copyright 2023, Refuge Enterprises LLC. All rights reserved.

"Especially when losses are traumatic, they may be difficult to discuss or even disclose to another. And yet the psychological and physical burden of harboring painful memories without the release of sharing can prove far more destructive in the long run."

Lessons of Loss: A Guide to Coping,
Dr. Robert Niemeyer

Tips for Journaling Through Grief

- There are no right or wrong answers.
- Mindfully engage with your whole being.
- Approach familiar subjects as if it were the first time.
- Walk up to the edge, but don't fall over.
- Seek out physical and emotional support as needed.
- Go through the journal in order. Or don't.

Heartfelt Thoughts

Today I am grateful for...
_____
_____
_____
_____
_____

I am hopeful for...
_____
_____
_____
_____
_____

Notes & Reminders:
_____
_____
_____
_____

Heartfelt Thoughts

Who have you lost? (friends, family, lovers, partners)

_____
_____
_____
_____
_____
_____

How did those losses change you and the story of your life?

_____
_____
_____
_____
_____
_____

Notes & Reminders:

_____
_____
_____
_____

Notes

Heartfelt Thoughts

Today I miss...

_____
_____
_____
_____
_____
_____

I remember when you and I....

_____
_____
_____
_____
_____
_____

Notes & Reminders:

_____
_____
_____
_____

Notes

I give myself time and space to feel all my feelings.

Heartfelt Thoughts

Today I am grateful for...

_____
_____
_____
_____
_____

I am hopeful for...

_____
_____
_____
_____
_____
_____

Notes & Reminders:

_____
_____
_____
_____

Heartfelt Thoughts

Some of my grief triggers are...

_____
_____
_____
_____
_____
_____

What feelings are challenging for me to confront?

_____
_____
_____
_____
_____
_____

Notes & Reminders:

_____
_____
_____

Notes

Heartfelt Thoughts

This is what I have to say to you....

_____
_____
_____
_____
_____
_____
_____

My happiest memory of you is...

_____
_____
_____
_____
_____
_____
_____

Notes & Reminders:

_____
_____
_____
_____

Notes

I always thought I wanted to be perfect, but my grief has taught me to be human instead.

Heartfelt Thoughts

Today I am grateful for...
_____
_____
_____
_____
_____

I am hopeful for...
_____
_____
_____
_____
_____

Notes & Reminders:
_____
_____
_____
_____

Heartfelt Thoughts

The first time I did ___ without you I....

_____
_____
_____
_____
_____
_____

The greatest lesson I have learned is...

_____
_____
_____
_____
_____
_____

Notes & Reminders:

_____
_____
_____
_____

Notes

Heartfelt Thoughts

When I feel upset, I can call...

___
___
___
___
___
___
___

Today, I remembered...

___
___
___
___
___
___
___

Notes & Reminders:

___
___
___
___

Notes

I know sadness and despair; I know failure and defeat. I also know courage and survival and humanity. Mine is a story of hope for someone (even if that someone is me).

Heartfelt Thoughts

Today I am grateful for...
_____
_____
_____
_____
_____

I am hopeful for...
_____
_____
_____
_____
_____
_____

Notes & Reminders:
_____
_____
_____
_____

Heartfelt Thoughts

This experience has taught me...
_____
_____
_____
_____
_____
_____

Do I have any regrets about this situation?
_____
_____
_____
_____
_____
_____

Notes & Reminders:
_____
_____
_____

Notes

Heartfelt Thoughts

What feelings am I looking forward to?
_____
_____
_____
_____
_____
_____

What feelings do I want to leave behind?
_____
_____
_____
_____
_____
_____

Notes & Reminders:
_____
_____
_____

Notes

My heart is big enough to hold everything I feel; everyone I've ever loved; every season of my life.

Heartfelt Thoughts

Today I am grateful for...
_____
_____
_____
_____
_____

I am hopeful for...
_____
_____
_____
_____
_____

Notes & Reminders:
_____
_____
_____
_____

Heartfelt Thoughts

What are some ways you've expressed grief in the past?
_____
_____
_____
_____
_____
_____
_____

Did they feel helpful to you?
_____
_____
_____
_____
_____
_____
_____

Notes & Reminders:
_____
_____
_____
_____

Notes

Heartfelt Thoughts

Do I feel comfortable asking for help?
_____
_____
_____
_____
_____
_____

Why or why not?
_____
_____
_____
_____
_____
_____

Notes & Reminders:
_____
_____
_____

Notes

Their breath become my own.
Their light become my own.
Their heart live on in mine.
Their life carry on through me.

Heartfelt Thoughts

Today I am grateful for...

_____

_____

_____

_____

_____

I am hopeful for...

_____

_____

_____

_____

_____

Notes & Reminders:

_____

_____

_____

_____

Heartfelt Thoughts

How did this person or experience make you feel?
_____
_____
_____
_____
_____
_____

What's a positive memory I have of this person or situation?
_____
_____
_____
_____
_____
_____

Notes & Reminders:
_____
_____
_____
_____

Notes

Make a list of a few different ways you can honor your loved one or your loss.

If you are grieving the loss of a person, write down a list of things specific to them that you admired.

I am grateful for the strength to carry their spirit forward into this new chapter.

Heartfelt Thoughts

Today I am grateful for...

_____
_____
_____
_____
_____

I am hopeful for...

_____
_____
_____
_____
_____
_____

Notes & Reminders:

_____
_____
_____
_____

Heartfelt Thoughts

Here are five ways I can be compassionate with myself today...

_____
_____
_____
_____
_____
_____

When I am overcome by grief, here is a mantra or affirmation I can use to comfort myself:

_____
_____
_____
_____
_____
_____

Notes & Reminders:

_____
_____
_____

Notes

Heartfelt Thoughts

Do I know anyone else who is grieving?
_____
_____
_____
_____
_____
_____

How can I try to make them feel better today?
_____
_____
_____
_____
_____
_____

Notes & Reminders:
_____
_____
_____
_____

Notes

If I must fall, I will rise each time a better person.

Heartfelt Thoughts

Today I am grateful for...

_____
_____
_____
_____
_____

I am hopeful for...

_____
_____
_____
_____
_____

Notes & Reminders:

_____
_____
_____
_____

Heartfelt Thoughts

What creative ways do I use to express my feelings?

_____
_____
_____
_____
_____
_____

If I can't think of any, what are some I can try?

_____
_____
_____
_____
_____
_____

Notes & Reminders:

_____
_____
_____

Notes

Heartfelt Thoughts

What song makes you think of your loved one?

___

Why?

___

Notes & Reminders:

___

Notes

When I look at my pain, I look with compassion. When I look into my past, I look with forgiveness. When I look inside myself, I look with patience. When I look at the world, I look for ways to give. When I look at my memories of you, I find you here with me still.

Heartfelt Thoughts

Today I am grateful for...

_____

_____

_____

_____

_____

I am hopeful for...

_____

_____

_____

_____

_____

Notes & Reminders:

_____

_____

_____

_____

Heartfelt Thoughts

My loved one used to say...

___

___

___

___

___

___

I don't ever want to forget...

___

___

___

___

___

___

Notes & Reminders:

___

___

___

Notes

Write a love letter to your loved one.

Notes

Notes

I may never be the same, but what I loved remains part of me.

Heartfelt Thoughts

Today I am grateful for...

_____
_____
_____
_____
_____
_____

I am hopeful for...

_____
_____
_____
_____
_____
_____

Notes & Reminders:

_____
_____
_____
_____

Heartfelt Thoughts

I am having a hard time with...

_____
_____
_____
_____
_____

I have been feeling a lot of...

_____
_____
_____
_____
_____

Notes & Reminders:

_____
_____
_____

Notes

Heartfelt Thoughts

The hardest time of day is...

_____
_____
_____
_____
_____

I am ready to feel...

_____
_____
_____
_____
_____

Notes & Reminders:

_____
_____
_____

Notes

Although life will never be the same, it can somehow still be good.

Heartfelt Thoughts

Today I am grateful for...

_____
_____
_____
_____
_____
_____

I am hopeful for...

_____
_____
_____
_____
_____
_____

Notes & Reminders:

_____
_____
_____
_____

If I could go back in time, I would do this differently.

Notes

What are my goals for the rest of my life?

Notes

I allow myself to feel my grief and then let go.

Heartfelt Thoughts

Today I am grateful for...

_____
_____
_____
_____
_____
_____

I am hopeful for...

_____
_____
_____
_____
_____
_____

Notes & Reminders:

_____
_____
_____
_____

Heartfelt Thoughts

I could use some more...

_____
_____
_____
_____
_____

I could use a little less...

_____
_____
_____
_____
_____

Notes & Reminders:

_____
_____
_____

Notes

Heartfelt Thoughts

A simple activity or non-activity I could try today to make things easier is...

___
___
___
___
___
___

I find it helpful when...

___
___
___
___
___
___

Notes & Reminders:

___
___
___

Notes

I will hold on to love and release the grief.

Heartfelt Thoughts

Today I am grateful for...

_____
_____
_____
_____
_____
_____
_____

I am hopeful for...

_____
_____
_____
_____
_____
_____
_____

Notes & Reminders:

_____
_____
_____
_____

Heartfelt Thoughts

I feel most connected to my loved one when I...

_____
_____
_____
_____
_____

My loved one had a way of making me feel...

_____
_____
_____
_____
_____
_____

Notes & Reminders:

_____
_____
_____

Notes

Heartfelt Thoughts

If I could be like my loved one in any way, I would adopt their...

_____
_____
_____
_____
_____

To be more compassionate toward myself, I am willing to try...

_____
_____
_____
_____
_____

Notes & Reminders:

_____
_____
_____

Notes

I can feel happy and hopeful today.

Heartfelt Thoughts

Today I am grateful for...

_____
_____
_____
_____
_____
_____

I am hopeful for...

_____
_____
_____
_____
_____
_____

Notes & Reminders:

_____
_____
_____

Heartfelt Thoughts

I feel most connected to my loved one when I...

_____
_____
_____
_____
_____

My loved one had a way of making me feel...

_____
_____
_____
_____
_____
_____

Notes & Reminders:

_____
_____
_____
_____

Notes

Heartfelt Thoughts

If I could be like my loved one in any way, I would adopt their...

_____
_____
_____
_____
_____

To be more compassionate toward myself, I am willing to try...

_____
_____
_____
_____
_____
_____

Notes & Reminders:

_____
_____
_____
_____

Notes

I can feel happy and hopeful today.

Heartfelt Thoughts

Today I am grateful for...
_____
_____
_____
_____
_____
_____

I am hopeful for...
_____
_____
_____
_____
_____
_____

Notes & Reminders:
_____
_____
_____

Heartfelt Thoughts

When I have intense feelings come up, where do I feel them in my body?

_____
_____
_____
_____
_____
_____

What is the hardest part of this process for me?

_____
_____
_____
_____
_____
_____

Notes & Reminders:

_____
_____
_____
_____

Notes

Heartfelt Thoughts

Have I ever struggled to give myself permission to fully grieve?

_____
_____
_____
_____
_____
_____

Why do I think that is?

_____
_____
_____
_____
_____
_____

Notes & Reminders:

_____
_____
_____

Notes

Notes

Notes

Notes

Notes

Notes

Notes

www.ingramcontent.com/pod-product-compliance
Lightning Source LLC
LaVergne TN
LVHW051956060526
838201LV00059B/3677